International Relations:

A Simple Introduction

Also by K.H. Erickson

Simple Introductions

Accounting and Finance Formulas
Choice Theory
Corporate Finance Formulas
eBay
Econometrics
Economics
Financial Economics
Financial Risk Management
Game Theory
Game Theory for Business
International Relations
Investment Appraisal
Investment Formulas
Marketing Management Concepts and Tools
Mathematical Formulas for Economics and Business
Methods of Microeconomics
Microeconomics

International Relations:

A Simple Introduction

K.H. Erickson

Contents

1 Introduction

International relations examines the issues and frameworks which states, institutions, groups and individuals face in the global arena. Focusing on political economy, and social, cultural or technological factors, the subject explores the role of interdependence and the distribution of power in international expectations and outcomes. This book looks at some of the central issues in international relations, investigating four different areas which can be examined individually but which also all link together to form a coherent and enlightening narrative.

First, the motivation for international trade is examined with the theory of the gains from trade. This looks at production and efficiency, and explains how countries may benefit by only producing goods where they hold a comparative advantage. But the gains from trade model is not without flaws and the forecasted gains may not occur in practice for a variety of reasons, which largely revolve around issues of power and interdependence among countries. The second area of the book explores this idea in greater depth, investigating the differing realist and liberal theories on the role of power and interdependence in international trade. The motivations behind the global trend toward liberalization and the removal of trade barriers between states are then examined, with two detailed case studies examining the decisive factors in the liberalizations of India and Mexico.

In the third area of focus the discussion of power and interdependence at the international level is escalated, with an investigation of the prospects for international cooperation on global issues. The ongoing international problem of global warming is explained, both in terms of its potentially catastrophic effects and the struggle to get states to take meaningful action beyond token gestures. This discussion reveals that states appear to treat greenhouse gas emissions and the associated global warming as a game, and this leads to the application of game theory models to the topic to bring a greater understanding of the forces at work. The challenge to get countries to reduce greenhouse gas emissions is explained and represented as an assurance game, prisoners' dilemma game, and a chicken game between the USA and China, currently the two biggest sources of greenhouse gas emissions. The applicability of each of the three types of game to the real world is then assessed, along with the associated implications for solving the problem of global warming.

The struggle to get different countries to come together leads on to the fourth and final topic to be investigated, and the impact which cultural difference between nation-states has upon international outcomes.

Communitarian, constructivist, and cosmopolitan theories of culture's role in international relations are explained, with each predicting international conflict, change, and unity respectively. Evidence supporting each theory is then examined, as a means to understand the possible causes of past, current and future events in the global arena.

2 Gains from Trade

2.1 Output without International Trade

Imagine that there are two different countries producing goods; country A and country B. And imagine that each of these countries only has two goods available for production; mobile phones or shirts. In this example country A has 1,000,000 workers, and each individual worker can either produce 5 mobile phones or 20 shirts per week. Country B has 100,000 workers, and each individual worker can either produce 50 mobile phones or 100 shirts per week.

Country A output

Looking first at the case of country A, if every one of its workers produced mobile phones then weekly output for country A would be calculated as follows:

1,000,000 workers producing phones
5 phones per worker per week

1,000,000 x 5 = **5,000,000 phones produced per week**

If every worker in country A instead produced shirts then its national output per week would be:

1,000,000 workers producing shirts
20 shirts per worker per week

1,000,000 x 20 = **20,000,000 shirts produced per week**

And if country A split its workers between mobile phones and shirts evenly, with 500,000 workers producing each of the two products, then weekly national output for country A would be calculated as follows:

500,000 workers producing phones
5 phones per worker per week

500,000 x 5 = **2,500,000 phones produced per week**

500,000 workers producing shirts
20 shirts per worker per week

500,000 x 20 = **10,000,000 shirts produced per week**

A production possibility frontier (PPF) can be used to show the above output numbers in a more illustrative visual form, and reveal the range of production opportunities available to country A in the default scenario without any international trade. The dashed straight line in the following diagram is the PPF, point x represents the situation where country A's workers only produce mobile phones, point y shows the case where workers all make shirts, and point z sees half the country's workers make shirts and the other half produce phones. The production possibility frontier also shows the output resulting from all other possible variations of worker shirt or mobile phone production, and the straight line shows all of the shirt and mobile phone maximum output combinations available to country A.

Country A production possibility frontier, with no trade

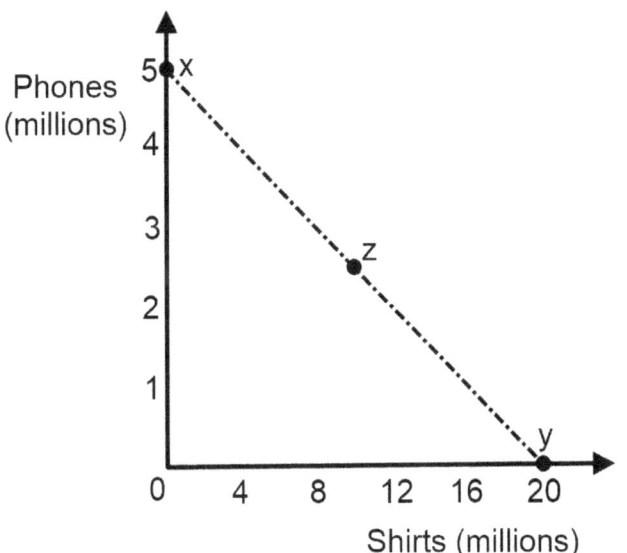

Country A's shirt and mobile phone production possibility frontier will be revisited in the next section, to assess the impact which international trade can have on a country's production and output potential. But first a production possibility frontier will be calculated and shown for the other country in this example, country B.

Country B output

Turning next to country B, if every worker in the country produced mobile phones then weekly output would be calculated as follows, using the numbers given at the start of this section:

100,000 workers producing phones
50 phones per worker per week

100,000 x 50 = **5,000,000 phones produced per week**

If every worker in country B was put to work producing shirts instead, then national output per week would be:

100,000 workers producing shirts
100 shirts per worker per week

100,000 x 100 = **10,000,000 shirts produced per week**

And if country B split its workers between mobile phones and shirts equally, with 50,000 of its workers producing phones and the other 50,000 workers making shirts, then country B's weekly output would be calculated as follows:

50,000 workers producing phones
50 phones per worker per week

50,000 x 50 = **2,500,000 phones produced per week**

50,000 workers producing shirts
100 shirts per worker per week

50,000 x 100 = **5,000,000 shirts produced per week**

Another production possibility frontier (PPF) diagram can illustrate these output numbers for country B. As before the dashed line in the diagram is the PPF, point x represents the situation where the country's workers only produce mobile phones, point y shows the case where all workers make shirts, and point z sees half of the country's workers make shirts and the other half produce phones. The production possibility frontier below also shows the output resulting from all other potential variations of worker shirt or phone production, and the shirt and phone maximum output combinations available to country B.

Country B production possibility frontier, with no trade

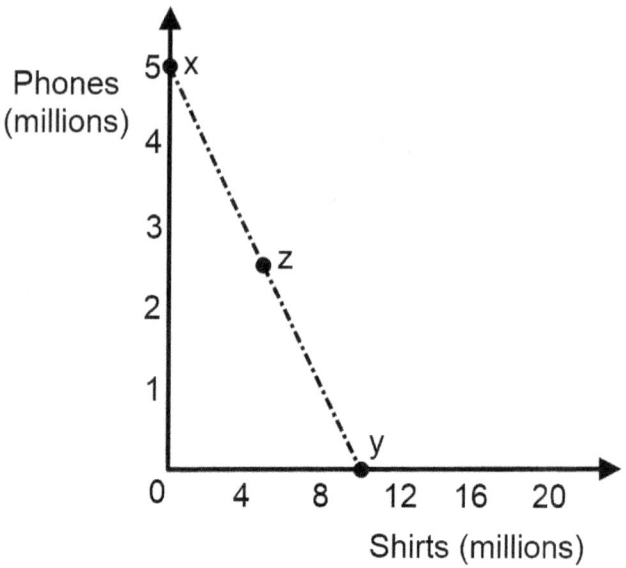

Country B's shirt and phone PPF will be revisited again in the next section, to account for the changes to output associated with international trade.

Total output without international trade

With output and production possibility frontiers for both country A and country B the total possible output can now be found for this example two country world. Country A could make 5,000,000 mobile phones per week if all of its workers were dedicated to the task, while country B could also make 5,000,000 phones per week if all of its workers made phones. This means the maximum possible mobile phone output here is as follows:

Country A weekly mobile phone production: 5,000,000
Country B weekly mobile phone production: 5,000,000

Maximum total weekly phone production
= 5,000,000 + 5,000,000
= 10,000,000 phones

And if all of country A's workers produced shirts then they would produce 20,000,000 shirts per week, while if all of country B's workers produced shirts they would make 10,000,000 shirts. This gives the following maximum possible shirt output:

Country A weekly shirt production: 20,000,000
Country B weekly shirt production: 10,000,000

Maximum total weekly shirt production
= 20,000,000 + 10,000,000
30,000,000 shirts

However, in the default scenario where there is no international trade country A and country B would be unlikely to focus all of their workers on the production of just one good. Each country would need to meet both their mobile phone and their shirt needs all by themselves, and produce each of the two goods themselves instead of relying on others for either shirts or phones. To keep things simple it will be assumed that each country will spilt its workers evenly (50/50) between mobile phone and shirt production to achieve this end, and this has already been calculated earlier and shown in the previous two PPF diagrams at point z. Point z for country A gave production output of 2,500,000 mobile phones per week and 10,000,000 shirts per week. Point z for country B sees production of 2,500,000 phones per week and 5,000,000 shirts per week. The total output of phones and shirts per week is therefore:

Country A weekly mobile phone production: 2,500,000
Country B weekly mobile phone production: 2,500,000

Total weekly phone production = 2,500,000 + 2,500,000 = 5,000,000 phones

Country A weekly shirt production: 10,000,000
Country B weekly shirt production: 5,000,000

Total weekly shirt production = 10,000,000 + 5,000,000 = 15,000,000 shirts

This is the total weekly output created by countries A and B if each country dedicates half of their workforce to producing shirts, and the other half to making shirts, in the default scenario where there isn't international trade between the two countries. These values will be revisited in the next section, to determine the effects which the addition of international trade has upon total output.

2.2 Output with International Trade

Common sense may suggest that a country would be better off avoiding international trade, like countries A and B in the last section, and instead producing all of the products it requires within its own borders. This would see it maintain independence and control of its national destiny, and avoid interdependency with other states which could put it in a vulnerable positon. But despite this logic countries worldwide engage in trade with all corners of the globe. This is motivated by the idea that there are significant benefits associated with international trading, known as the gains from trade. These theoretical gains are based on the idea that some countries are more efficient than others in a certain field of production, and that a state can gain greater output by letting a more efficient country produce a desired good and acquiring it via international trade, than by producing that good themselves.

Efficiency in production

If a country can produce a certain good using fewer units of input resources than other countries require then it is absolutely more efficient at production of that good. And a country is relatively more efficient in the production of a good than other countries if it has a lower opportunity cost, defined as the level of output which would have been achieved by the next best alternative use of production inputs.

Returning to the example of country A and country B from the last section, each worker in country A was revealed to be able to produce either 5 phones or 20 shirts per week. And each worker in country B was noted to be able to produce either 50 phones or 100 shirts per week. With a worker, which can be seen as one unit of an input resource, in country B able to produce more production output of either good per week than country A, *country B is absolutely more efficient in the production of both mobile phones and shirts*. This may appear to suggest that country B has nothing to gain from international trade, but it is too early to draw conclusions.

To determine which country is relatively more efficient in production each country's opportunity costs must be calculated. As noted in the definition of opportunity costs just given, this represents the level of output associated with the best alternative use of resource inputs (i.e. workers in this example).

Country A opportunity costs

A worker from country A can either produce 5 mobile phones or 20 shirts per week, and this ratio of 5 phones to

20 shirts therefore gives the following opportunity costs of production for country A:

Opportunity cost of 1 phone = 20/5 = 4 shirts
Opportunity cost of 1 shirt = 5/20 = 0.25 phones

The same process can then be repeated for country B to find its opportunity costs.

Country B opportunity costs

A worker in country B can produce either 50 phones or 100 shirts per week, for the following opportunity costs:

Opportunity cost of 1 phone = 100/50 = 2 shirts
Opportunity cost of 1 shirt = 50/100 = 0.5 phones

Comparative advantage in production

These two results for country A and country B reveal that country B has a lower opportunity cost of phone production. Putting one worker on phone production only sacrifices the production of 2 shirts for country B, while country A must sacrifice double that and misses out on the production of 4 shirts for every one worker it uses for phone production. Therefore *country B is relatively more efficient in the production of mobile phones.*

With shirts it is country A which has the lower opportunity cost of production. Using one of its workers for shirt production involves giving up the production of 0.25 phones for country A, and this is half the production output of 0.5 phones which country B must sacrifice by using one of its own workers for shirt production. Therefore *country A is relatively more efficient in the production of shirts*.

When a country is relatively more efficient in the production of a good it is said to have a comparative advantage in that field. Therefore *country A has a comparative advantage in shirt production*, and *country B has a comparative advantage in mobile phone production*. The fact that country B is absolutely more efficient in the production of both shirt and mobile phone goods than country A, and can produce more units of output per worker, is irrelevant here. As will soon be made clear only the relative efficiency of production, determined by the sacrificed output of one good following the use of required resources for the production of a different good within the same country, decides a country's comparative advantage in production. With the two different countries A and B each having a comparative advantage in the production of a different good it makes sense for each to focus only on that good. Country A should only produce shirts, and country B should only produce mobile phones.

Total output with comparative advantage specialization

If both countries followed their comparative advantage specialization then all 1,000,000 of country A's workers would make shirts at their work rate of 20 shirts per worker per week, and all 100,000 of country B's workers would make phones at their work rate of 50 phones per week. This will result in total production output at:

Country A weekly shirt production = 1,000,000 x 20
= 20,000,000 shirts

Country B weekly phone production = 100,000 x 50
= 5,000,000 phones

These numbers can be compared to the total weekly output for the countries found at the end of section 2.1, when each country produced both shirts and phones with 50% of their workers producing each good. The weekly mobile phone production of 5,000,000 mobile phones is the same as before, but the weekly shirt production has increased from 15,000,000 when both countries made them to 20,000,000 when only country A produces shirts, talking advantage of its comparative advantage in the field. The result of each country specializing in the production of what they are best at increases the total weekly shirt output by 1/3 (5,000,000 shirts), without causing any loss in the output of mobile phones:

Total weekly phone output without specialization
= 5,000,000 phones
Total weekly phone output with specialization
= 5,000,000 phones (= no change)

Total weekly shirt output without specialization
= 15,000,000 phones
Total weekly shirt output with specialization
= 20,000,000 phones (= +33.33%)

However, if country A and B specialize in production according to their individual comparative advantages then by definition they give up on the production of the other good, and this will leave each country without access to either shirts or phones. If country A only makes shirts then it will lack natural access to mobile phones, and if country B only produces mobile phones then it will not have natural access to shirts. The only way to resolve this situation in this example two country world, and the only way for country A to acquire mobile phones and for country B to acquire shirts, is for the two countries producing different goods to trade with each other. But before this international trade can proceed terms must be agreed between the two theoretical states.

Terms of trade

In order for international trade to occur between two countries terms of trade must first be determined. These terms of trade are simply the price that each country will pay for the good they want to import, and the price each country will receive for the good they produce and seek to export. Terms of trade are calculated as the ratio of export prices to import prices.

If country A specializes in production according to comparative advantage then it will only produce shirts, and will seek to gain mobile phones via imports from country B. And country A will naturally want favourable terms of trade and as low a price as possible for these mobile phone imports. If country B specializes in production according to comparative advantage then it will only produce mobile phones, and will seek to gain shirts via imports from country A. And country B will naturally also seek terms of trade which are in their favour, and it will want as low a price as possible for these shirt imports.

Acceptable terms of trade for both countries

Acceptable terms of trade for each of the two countries would simply be those which offer a better price, i.e. a lower opportunity cost, than they faced without trade. For example, country A's own opportunity cost per phone was noted earlier to be 4 shirts, so it would only accept terms of trade which see 1 mobile phone cost less than 4 of its shirts. And country B's own opportunity cost per shirt is 0.5 phones, and it would only trade if 1 shirt cost less than 0.5 of its phones. Putting the two requirements together shows that acceptable terms of trade for both countries is for 2 shirts to cost less than 1 phone (i.e. 1 shirt costs less than 0.5 phones, to meet country B's requirement), and for 1 phone to cost less than 4 shirts (which sees 0.25 phones cost less than 1 shirt) to satisfy country A's requirement. The details are summarized below:

2 shirts < <u>1 phone</u> < 4 shirts
0.25 phones < <u>1 shirt</u> < 0.5 phones

International trade expands production possibilities

Terms of trade which price 1 phone at equivalent to 3 shirts and 1 shirt equivalent to 0.333 phones, for example, would be acceptable to both country A and country B according to the above requirements, and would motivate international trade. With this example price country A could either hold on to the 20,000,000 shirts it produces per week by following its comparative advantage production specialization, or trade all of it with country B to gain 6,666,667 phones per week (= 20 * 0.333), or trade only some of their shirts to end up between one of these two extremes. The following diagram shows the effect that these terms of trade would have on the production possibility frontier (PPF) of country A introduced earlier, and highlights the gains from trade.

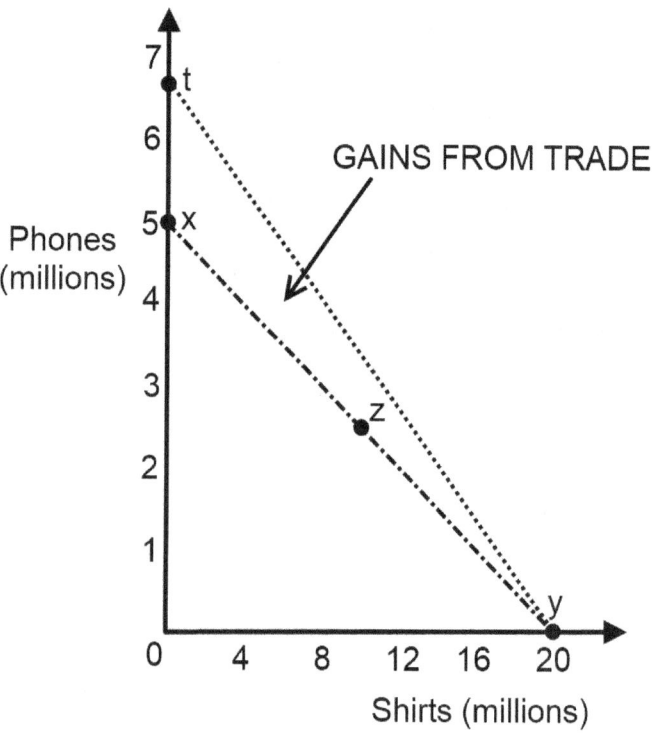

Country A production possibility frontier, with international trade

The example terms of trade of 1 phone to 3 shirts has expanded the PPF outwards from dashed line y to x when it didn't trade, to the new dotted line of point y to point t (with 6,666,667 phones). Every point on this new PPF, except for point y where country A has no interest in phones and holds on to all 20,000,000 of its produced shirts, shows greater output than the original PPF. And therefore if country A has any interest in phones whatsoever it makes sense to let country B use its comparative advantage and produce all of the phones, and country A should only get them via trade. In simple terms trade opens up production possibilities to country A which it could never achieve on its own, the difference between the dashed and dotted lines in the diagram, labelled as gains from trade.

Trade offers similar benefits to country B. With 1 shirt priced equal to 0.333 phones and 1 phone priced at 3 shirts, country B could either hold onto the 5,000,000 mobile phones it produced with its comparative advantage production specialization, or trade them all with country A to gain 15,000,000 shirts in return, or anywhere in between these extremes. The following diagram revisits the PPF of country B seen earlier and notes the effect of international trade, and as with country A trade expands the production possibilities outwards. The new PPF is the dotted line between point x and point t (with 15,000,000 shirts), replacing the original PPF shown by the dashed line between points x and y. Every point on this new production possibilities frontier shows greater output than the original, except for point x where country B has no interest in shirts and keeps all of the 5,000,000 mobile phones it produced. Therefore if country B has any interest in shirts it should let country A make them all and only get them via international trade, to benefit from greater production. The production possibilities increase for country B here is the difference between the dashed and dotted line in the diagram, labelled as gains from trade.

Country B production possibility frontier, with international trade

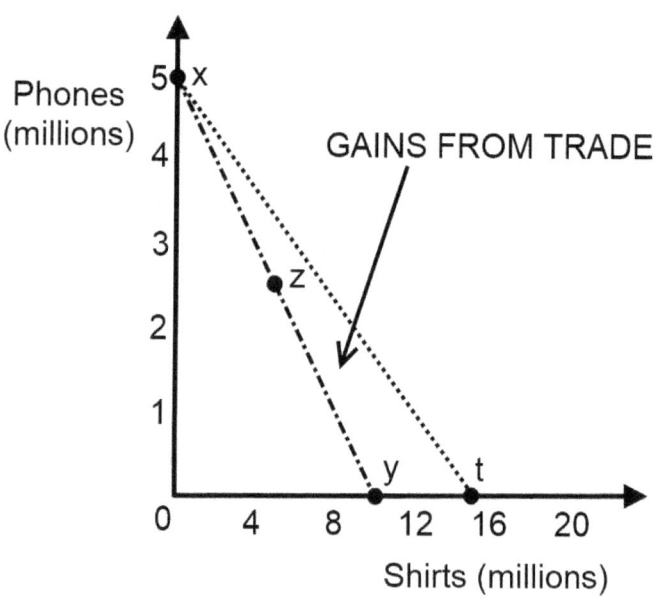

2.3 Flaws in Gains from Trade Theory

The simple example put forward in the last section saw countries specialize in production according to their comparative advantage, gaining access to alternative goods via international trade, and being rewarded with greater production and output possibilities for doing so. However, this idea of gains from trade is only a theory and it may not occur in practice for a number of reasons.

Putting workers' needs before output growth

The gains from trade theory assumes that the only thing a country would or should care about is a comparative advantage in production, and opportunities for greater output, but in practice a country will of course care about the specific needs of its workers. The government of any democratic country depends on workers for votes, and openly outsourcing all jobs in unproductive sectors to other countries may be incredibly unpopular, and could cost the government re-election. This can explain why a country may choose not to follow its comparative advantage.

Even if a country does follow its comparative advantage the whole idea of gains from trade can fall apart if other countries don't hold to their side of the bargain. A country won't be able to make the most of its comparative advantage in trade if the cost and price of their products is artificially raised by other countries, who may create high import tariffs to protect their nation's workers from being undercut by more efficient international producers.

Market uncertainty

Another flaw with gains from trade theory is that it is assumed that the market in which trades are conducted is efficient, but this is based on the assumption that market trades are a barter over goods' value (i.e. the terms of trade) between only two sides. In reality things will be more complicated than this. In practice there will be far more than two participants determining the terms of trade and the number of participants can change over time, while the interaction will not involve a barter over goods with inherent value but will use money currency as the measure of value, which is subject to fluctuating exchange rates. In simple terms the comparative advantage model assumes simple static factors (the number of participants and the good's value), but real life trades are dynamic in nature and often unpredictable, and any gains from trade could therefore disappear in a short time period.

A related issue is that countries themselves may ensure that gains from trade are short-lived, with risk averse behaviour which tries to manage the unpredictability just noted. Once a country has secured a comparative advantage and the associated gains from trade it may set high import tariffs on those goods, to protect the industries and profits which its national income depends upon from changing external factors, which could empower competitors at their expense. But such tariff setting behaviour goes against the spirit of free trade underlying the comparative advantage model, and may invite a tit-for-tat response from other countries who may set their own high import tariffs to erode the gains from trade.

Developing countries may struggle to gain from trade

Developing countries may find it particularly difficult to benefit from trade. The process of gaining from trade will often involve significant change and social disruption in a country, and workers may need to be retrained for different and more productive sectors to follow the country's comparative advantage. Workers may therefore require unemployment benefits for a period of time, while the employers which invest in retraining workers will require subsidies to cover their investment. But while richer Western countries may be able to afford these benefits and subsidies less wealthy developing countries may not, and therefore they may find themselves unable to make the transition required to gain from trade.

Another major flaw with the gains from trade comparative advantage model is that it assesses efficiency in production solely based on workers' labour, ignoring the fact that some sectors are far more lucrative than others. And unfortunately for developing countries they're more likely to be involved with the latter. Poorer developing countries often try to focus on a comparative advantage in simple agricultural products, often due to the lack of resources required to retrain workers for more advanced sectors as just noted, while richer Western countries instead focus on the more expensive production of cars, electronics, machinery, or advanced manufactured products such as pharmaceuticals. As a result developing countries may find that the value of their exports are dwarfed by the money spent on imports, leaving them with permanent adverse terms of trade (the ratio of export prices to import prices). This may ensure that gains from trade are one-sided as all the gains go to other countries at the expense of developing nations.

And developing countries are also more at risk from significant changes in the terms of trade, caused by large increases in output from one major supplier or changes in output by large numbers of traders, due to their common dependence on only a few low value products. Wealthier countries can insulate against industry risk by focusing on a range of different products so a downturn in one area is balanced out by upturns in other fields, and their trade is often based on high profits per unit which naturally allows for some leeway. But developing countries may lack the resources to get involved in a range of industries to hedge industry risk, and their profits are often based on trading high quantities of units with a low profit per unit, leaving them far more vulnerable to price fluctuations. Overall the idea of gains from trade may therefore apply far more to richer countries than poorer ones, as opposed to being a robust universal model.

Developing countries hoped that the World Trade Organization (WTO) could improve their experience with international trade, and give access to new wealthy markets for their products. However, the consensus decision making and group diplomacy which typifies the WTO has often worked against developing countries, as it ignores the fact that some countries have greater power and resources than others, and this strengthens the position of the wealthiest countries at poorer countries' expense. All countries will naturally seek what is best for their own nation, and this may result in a desire for high domestic tariffs to protect their own workers from foreign imports, and low or zero international tariffs to allow them to maximize export sales. And the WTO has often functioned simply as a tool for the wealthiest countries to achieve this goal and push their will on developing countries, with what has been known as 'dirty tariffication'. This is where developed countries subsidize their domestic agriculture to create the equivalent of tariffs at a level which foreign imports can't compete with, while at the same time also producing a surplus of products to flood other countries with exports priced low enough to succeed in developing countries' markets.

As noted at the start of section 2.2, international trade can put countries in a vulnerable interdependent position, and it's no surprise that developed countries may seek to protect themselves and their powerful historic position. The role of interdependence and power in trade is examined in further depth in the next chapter.

3 Trade Liberalization, Power & Interdependence

3.1 Realist and Liberal Models of International Trade

Chapter 2 suggested that international trade and the international political system are decided by the power and interdependence of the participants, but the precise role these factors play in countries' interactions is disputed by rival political theories. The realist and liberal models of international politics have different ideas on the workings of the global system, and of the influences motivating the global trend toward the liberalization of trade, deregulation, and submitting to global market forces.

Realist theory

Realist theory believes that the central units of the international political system are sovereign nation-states, and that the absence of an impartial global authority to keep all countries in line (e.g. a world government) means global politics is organized as an anarchy. The basic idea is that without a top-down rule of law imposed and enforced fairly across the world nation-states have no choice but to look after their own individual interests, as no one else will. Under realist theory interdependence between countries is too risky and a non-starter, as it could interfere with a country's main goal of self-preservation if other countries were to turn on them at some point in the future. Therefore product specialization according to comparative advantage is out of the question, as it is based upon interdependence between states. With countries unable to compete using product differentiation, according to realist theory, they can only differentiate themselves based on relative power. And therefore countries must defend any power advantage they possess, as if other nation-states are allowed to gain power at their expense it could be used to gain control over them, and threaten their existence.

With various forms of trade specialization visible across the world the validity of realist political theory may immediately appear in question, but adherents to realism would see things differently. Realists would insist that it is not mutual production gains via interdependence which motivates such specialization but relative power gains, and that outsourcing certain industries to other countries is not an interdependent act but instead a self-interested act. For example, relying on developing countries to produce textiles would be seen as encouraging and imposing a low skilled and low paid role onto workers of those countries.

The goal being to ensure that developing nations don't advance toward high skilled and high paid work, as that may threaten the position of the wealthiest and most developed countries which currently enjoy that role, and which want to keep it that way to hold on to their relative position of power.

Liberal theory

Liberal theory agrees with realism that sovereign states are the core units of international politics, and that the global system is anarchic in nature due to the absence of a supranational world government. But while realism believes that states are always focused on international survival, liberal theory argues that the interests which states pursue internationally ultimately depend on the internal politics and dominant individuals and groups in a country, which may change over time. Liberals agree that states will seek out power, but see a potential for countries to put relative power concerns aside in pursuit of individual absolute power gains in certain circumstances. The theory sees international interdependence as a possibility if the dominant groups in different countries agree that cooperation, and trade liberalization to open up trade borders, is in their own best interests, and that this incentive can motivate strategic interdependence in trade.

Returning to the example of developed states outsourcing textile production to developing countries, liberal theory would point to internal groups in the respective countries as the driving feature. Whether it is individual Western capitalists looking for greater profits and power by taking advantage of lower worker costs in the developing world, or factory owners in those countries seeking profits in the West off the back of the hard work of their compatriots, the focus is micro and not macro level decisions.

3.2 India Case Study

India provides an interesting case study to use to investigate issues of power and interdependence in trade liberalization, and to assess alternative realist and liberal political theories.

India pre-liberalization

Before their fully liberalizing trade reforms of the 1990s India was a mixed welfare economy, where state economic guidance and welfare was combined with aspects of a partially liberalized (since the 1980s) market economy. The country had a long history of state-centred protectionist import substitution, producing its own goods in place of foreign imports to maintain its independence, and the number of households living a subsistence livelihood was substantial. But a decision was made that India's dependence on low value agricultural exports was no longer acceptable, and that a policy of rapid industrialization was required to allow India to compete more effectively globally and to generate greater wealth for the country. And the goal of rapid industrialization required India to open up more to the world.

As trade liberalization naturally involves the reduction of welfare subsidies and economic guidance quotas, and the reduction of tariffs blocking foreign imports from challenging domestic producers, it therefore involved a major shakeup of the established system in India. This shakeup promised great opportunities for those who could make the most of it but also significant risks to those who couldn't, and with a large percentage of the Indian population already struggling on a subsistence livelihood there was a risk that major trade reforms could have a polarizing and divisive effect within India.

Realist explanations for India's trade liberalization

The original limited trade liberalization which had occurred in 1980s India is seen by realists as an attempt to halt the economic slowdown at the time, and avoid the risk associated with falling behind other countries. Partial liberalization and greater trade could in theory give access to the foreign technology required to raise the efficiency of domestic import substitution policies, while the state protected Indian workers from the worst aspects and risks of free trade and full liberalization. But then came the fall of the Soviet Union in the early 1990s and the triumph of free market global capitalism over the insular state run model, and India's global positon had changed. No longer could India positon itself between the West and the Soviets, picking and choosing from market and state economy models, and India was forced to reassess its international position. Realists would argue that India made the only choice it could to avoid powerless isolation, joining the winning side with a progression to full liberalization for a share of capitalist power.

Although India's major 1990s trade reforms were likely to be controversial to many inside the country Indian officials pushed ahead with the agreements, and realists highlight some major macro level concerns and global pressures on India at the time as an explanation. By 1990 it was clear that India was less efficient than it could be, despite the 1980s move to partial liberalization. More liberalized East Asian countries such as South Korea and Indonesia had similar levels of output yet they achieved this output with far lower shares of investment and employment than India's state owned enterprises required (Bromley et al., 2004). India's lower levels of efficiency than other Asian countries suggested lower rates of growth, and in the long-run that would see India's relative power position on the international stage decline, and according to realism that would threaten the country's survival. India therefore needed to change its strategy to be able to compete more effectively internationally and maintain its independence, and the example to follow had been set by the more liberalized and more efficient East Asian countries such as South Korea and Indonesia.

Realists also see another macro level factor as driving India's policy of trade liberalization in the 1990s, and that was the power that the International Monetary Fund (IMF) had over the country. India's 1980s partial liberalization and its import of foreign products to improve technology, efficiency and growth had come at a significant cost, and it resulted in a balance of payments crisis where the value of imports outstripped the value of exports, and more money was leaving India than entering the country. Under realist theory such a situation is intolerable as it empowered rival states at India's expense, and India asked the IMF for a loan to make up its deficit and resolve the problem. The loan was granted, but one of the conditions which the IMF attached to the loan was that India must follow the IMF's value system, and fully liberalize itself to market forces. The IMF argued that this was in India's best interests, based on the logic of the comparative advantage theory put forward in chapter 2. But realists would see a more nefarious motive behind the IMF demand that countries must fully liberalize to market forces. In the IMF voting power is assigned based on a country's relative position in the world economy, and this essentially means that the wealthiest and most powerful countries decide IMF policy. Helping other countries become wealthy and more powerful would only threaten this privilege, and realism may therefore argue that the wealthiest countries' IMF demands were an attempt to ensure their relative power position was preserved, by bringing India further into a system where they could be better controlled.

However, although realist international theory may offer a range of plausible explanations why India agreed to go along with full trade liberalization in the early 1990s, realism alone can't explain why the actual implementation of various trade reforms has been constantly resisted and delayed over the following decades. But liberal international theory does offer some additional insights in this area, and it sees different factors as responsible for India's policies on liberalization.

Liberal explanations for India's trade liberalization

Liberal international theory is more concerned with internal factors in a country than external factors between states, and it sees the Indian government's struggle and conflict with groups inside the country as the cause of the delays in implementing trade agreements. Liberals also see the same factors as a major driver for the fully liberalizing trade agreements in the first place, and they would highlight the growing domestic problems in India in 1991 when the newly elected Indian government came into power. India was in the middle of an economic crisis, confidence was waning in the established socialist and nationalist state model following the collapse of communism, and the rise of the rival right-wing Hindu nationalist Bharatiya Janata Party (BJP) risked threatening the historically secular nature of Indian politics. Trade liberalization promised a solution to all of these problems according to liberal theory. Liberalization could empower and create new opportunities for the professional middle classes who had lost their dominance after the country's increased democratic participation, to drive India out of its economic crisis, and those who had lost faith in nationalist state socialism would have an alternative to follow which could rival the BJP. While there was some domestic opposition to liberalization and fears over the negative side effects there was far more fear about the growth of the BJP, and reform agreements pushed ahead to try to counteract this threat.

Groups which were gaining power and influence before full trade liberalization, such as those newly participating in democracy and the BJP, naturally had concerns that the reforms could reverse their power gains. And liberal international theory believes that delays in implementing the agreed trade reforms are down to getting everyone in India on board with the changes. There has been a general belief that there must be internal agreement, unity and interdependence before India is strong enough to manage the harsher but potentially the most beneficial IMF reforms, and implementation has often been slow as moving past internal conflict to foster that agreement among various groups has taken many years. Liberal theory believes that greater interdependence at the domestic level can facilitate greater power at the national level, and that this can explain the efforts India has made in that direction.

Liberal theory vs realist theory on India's liberalization

The harsher IMF reforms have ultimately been implemented in India in recent years, based on the idea that they will have the biggest impact on India's economic gains and growth, which may appeal to all groups within the country. National growth may in turn create greater relative power at the national level, which could result in more absolute power for groups at the local level, which relates back to realist international theory and the idea that relative power at the level of the nation-state is the most important thing. But the implementation of India's trade reforms only went ahead after changing internal circumstances, which eventually allowed greater internal interdependence and agreement on absolute gains for different groups, which supports the bottom-up liberal international theory that internal groups in a country and interdependence drive policy.

Overall the case study of India reveals that international trade depends on both internal and external factors in a country, on both interdependence and power, and that liberal and realist international theory each have an explanatory role to play. In India's case power and interdependence appear to have had a complementary relationship, and eventual interdependence between groups inside the country has allowed Indians to focus on gaining power internationally. It also appears that mutual absolute gains have ultimately been the most important factor in motivating India's move toward reform implementation and international interdependence in trade policy, trumping fears over potential relative losses, and perhaps giving more credence to liberal international theory than realist theory in this case.

3.3 Mexico Case Study

Mexico's trade liberalization story has much in common with that of India, but its motivations are different enough to make a separate case study worthwhile.

Mexico pre-liberalization

Mexico moved toward full trade liberalization agreements in the 1990s, based on the realization that insular state-driven industrialization and import substitution wouldn't create the economic growth the country required. As with the India case study, Mexico had first moved toward freer trade with partial liberalization in the 1980s in search of the well-documented benefits, and the 1990s liberalization reforms built on this process. The specifics of Mexico are very different however, due to the presence of the powerful United States of America just over its Northern border, and the lack of trust many Mexicans had in their government.

Liberal explanations for Mexico's trade liberalization

The liberal theory of international politics believes that internal factors drove Mexico's trade reforms in the 1990s. At the time the Mexican populace had lost trust and belief in both the nationalist PRI (Partido Revolucionario Institucional, or Institutional Revolutionary Party), and the corporatism model where the state allocates certain groups a monopoly of representation for various sectors of importance, in return for the influence of their leaders and policies. Unemployment, worker marginalization, and social conflict had all risen, and accusations of fraud both at home and abroad in the United States added to the challenge to the legitimacy of then Mexican president Carlos Salinas de Gortari. Further liberalization and free trade agreements with the United States, and the North American Free trade Agreement (NAFTA) in particular, was the perfect solution according to liberal international theory, as it locked domestic reforms into international agreements and took take the spotlight of Mexican citizens away from the Mexican government.

But liberals believe that Mexico's signing of NAFTA in the 1990s was primarily motivated by the absolute gains on offer from trade interdependence, based on the gains from trade idea first put forward in chapter 2. Closer ties and greater interdependence with an economy the size of the United States was thought to offer clear and significant benefits to Mexico at the time, as the USA was a huge market to export Mexican products to, while consumers could benefit from a better deal on a vast range of American imports. And followers of liberal theory would point to the large increases in Mexican exports over the twenty plus years since NAFTA came into force on 1st January 1994, to support this idea of mutually beneficial international interdependence.

Realist explanations for Mexico's trade liberalization

Realist international theory disagrees with liberal theory on Mexico's trade liberalization. It argues that Mexico's liberalization was not a willing move toward mutually beneficial trade interdependence for absolute gains, whether for the then president or Mexican producers, but instead a desperate move motivated by a desire to preserve Mexico's relative national power position in the global arena. Realism followers would point to the words of then Mexican president Salinas himself, who stated that Mexico needed to be a part of an economic trade bloc with the United States and Canada to remain attractive to investors (Bromley et al., 2004). The 1994 North American Free Trade Agreement (NAFTA) represented this economic trade bloc, and the talk of a need to remain attractive to investors was referring to the free trade agreement which the United States and Canada had signed in 1988, and which excluded other countries including Mexico. It appears that a major concern of the Mexican leadership which signed NAFTA was that the United States, the world's biggest economy and last remaining superpower, would focus on greater trade (and therefore power) ties with its Northern neighbour Canada alone, which would naturally reduce trade (and power) ties with other countries such as Mexico. And realist theory would argue that Mexico had to focus on relative trade levels and by implication relative power levels with the dominant USA, as its national survival depended upon it.

While there are clearly signs of interdependence present in the forming of the NAFTA economic trading bloc, as supporters of liberal theory point to, realists would insist that it is an asymmetric interdependence based on uneven power relations between the nation-states involved. The idea is that the United States naturally had significant power over Mexico, due to the vast economic power differential between the two countries, and the fact that Mexico needed trade with the US more than the US needed trade with Mexico. The American possession of vast power over a dependent Mexico meant the United States held go-it-alone power in any interdependent interaction, and could therefore interact however it wanted without fear of losing its relative power position. This meant the United States essentially held coercive power over Mexico, and either the latter accepted the NAFTA trade deal on the table, whether they liked it or not, or the US could focus on the existing trade deal with Canada which excluded Mexico. And in doing so impose unacceptable costs on the Mexican state by depriving them of essential trade.

Realists may cast doubt on the supposed absolute gains of the NAFTA trade deal for Mexico over the last twenty years, to disprove the liberal idea that it was absolute gains which motivated Mexico's liberalization and not relative gains. Realists would highlight the fact that NAFTA has not created clear absolute gains in the important areas of economic growth, productivity, job creation, wage levels, and discouragement of emigration in Mexico (Foreign Affairs, 2014). And although Mexico's exports have vastly increased in the twenty plus years since NAFTA came into force on the first day of 1994, over 70% of Mexico's exports are to the Unites States alone (Observatory of Economic Complexity, 2014). Realists see this as evidence that NAFTA has not offered absolute gains to Mexico so much as it has created relative gains, by tying it ever closer to the United States and allowing it to share in its relative successes, rather than becoming stronger in absolute terms and exporting more worldwide. NAFTA also imposed a major absolute cost on Mexico and it forced an amendment of the Mexican constitution, as some of it was incompatible with NAFTA. This also casts some doubt on the idea of absolute gains.

Liberal theory vs realist theory on Mexico's liberalization

The Mexican government has certainly benefitted from being able to tie domestic policies to international agreements, and NAFTA has drastically increased the level of Mexican producers' exports, to support the liberal international model which argues that internal groups in a country drive international policy and the move toward liberalization. But the words of the Mexican president Carlos Salinas de Gortari when NAFTA was implemented in 1994, and the focus on not being excluded from US trade blocs, shows that an external focus on relative power at the national level was a driving factor in liberalization, to support realist international theory.

Overall the case study of Mexico shows that liberal and realist theory can each support a greater understanding of the causes of liberalization, that both internal and external factors made a difference, and that both power and interdependence issues were present. However, unlike in the last case study with India the roles of power and interdependence appear to be contradictory and conflicting with Mexico. It was Mexico's lack of power relative to the United States which drove it toward an agreement which increased interdependence with the US, but on the other hand this stronger association has reinforced Mexico's sovereignty and offered a form of power. It appears that relative gains in international position, by forming stronger ties with the US, was ultimately the driving factor in Mexico's trade liberalization, giving more credence to realist theory than liberal international theory in this case. Liberal theory argues that countries may ignore the risk of relative losses at the international level in the pursuit of mutual absolute gains for domestic groups within those nation-states, but in the case of Mexico the opposite scenario may be closer to the truth. And Mexico may have ignored the risk of absolute losses domestically in terms of sacrificed economic growth, productivity, and jobs, in search of relative gains at the international level by forging far closer ties with the vastly more powerful USA.

4 The Games of International Relations

4.1 The Problem of Global Warming

Chapter 3 showed that power and independence can play a significant role in interactions at the domestic or national level, and this chapter develops this idea to evaluate the role these factors can play in the prospects for international cooperation on crucial global issues. Global warming and climate change have become an increasing concern in countries across the world, and the process sees various greenhouse gases (GHGs) in the atmosphere raise the earth's temperature, which in turn is thought to cause a number of changes to the earth's climate. While the sun's light and warming energy is required to sustain life on earth and a basic 'greenhouse effect' is therefore natural and essential, most scientists argue that human activity has caused the level of GHGs in the atmosphere to rise, and to in turn create an enhanced greenhouse effect which could have catastrophic consequences for life on earth. The possible negative consequences of this enhanced greenhouse effect, more commonly referred to as global warming, are thought to include significant changes to climate which could have the following effects:

1) Rising sea levels as higher temperatures cause an expansion of ocean water and melt ice caps, to threaten coastal communities;

2) Changing ocean salinity (salt levels), which can alter the water cycle and cause extreme weather conditions such as floods, droughts, or hurricanes;

3) Increased risk of rapid unexpected climate changes;

4) Greatly increased rates of species extinction, as species struggle to adapt to changing climates and habitats, which can have knock-on effects on the food chain and other species;

5) Growing migration levels as people struggle to cope with a changed environment and seek out a new one;

6) Global spread of diseases which are currently limited to only tropical climates (Bromley et al., 2004).

As the increased prevalence of damaging GHGs in the earth's atmosphere is blamed on human activity which occurs all across the world, such as agriculture using large numbers of cows which release methane into the atmosphere, and the burning of petrol to drive vehicles, global warming can't be stopped by any single country alone. Global warming and the climate change it causes instead require worldwide collective action, which acknowledges that global warming is what is known as a 'public good' (or a public bad to be more accurate), and exhibits two main features accordingly: it is non-rival and non-excludable. Non-rival means that a country can't offload the negative effects of global warming onto others, as one country's suffering doesn't reduce the suffering of others; and non-excludable means that no country can avoid the negative effects of global warming after it begins. These two features make global warming distinct from many other global concerns, and together they ensure that the only way for a country to protect itself from the negative effects of future global warming is to ensure that all, or at least most, other countries reduce GHG emissions.

The failure to reduce greenhouse gas emissions

Global warming and the resulting climate change has been a well-known and well-publicized problem for a long time, but there has been a notable lack of action to resolve it. While the damage that chlorofluorocarbons (CFCs) caused to the ozone layer was resolved with the 1980s Montreal Protocol international treaty, as countries worldwide agreed to phase out CFCs for more ozone friendly alternatives, the damage to the earth's climate caused by agriculture related methane and from burning fossil fuels continues on a massive scale. And the type of efforts seen with the elimination of CFCs remains elusive.

November 2014 agreements on the reduction of GHG emissions may appear to have finally started the resolution of the global warming problem, as the world's two biggest polluters China and the USA agreed to reduce their emissions. This followed an agreement a month earlier by the European Union countries (together the third biggest GHG emitter) to also reduce GHG emissions. But closer inspection of the agreements reveals their limitations.

China, the world's largest emitter of greenhouse gases by some distance, didn't mention any intention to reduce their current levels of GHG emissions which are the highest in the world, and only stated that their emission levels after the year 2030 would be lower than those which will occur in 2030. And even this agreement won't necessarily stand as the Chinese president who agreed it, Xi Jinping, is limited to two five years terms in office at the most, and having been elected to the presidency in 2013 he will be out of office by 2023 at the latest. The next Chinese president could decide that he wants to take China in a different direction, and renounce his predecessor's international agreement on GHG emissions.

The United States, currently the second largest emitter of GHGs, agreed to cut emissions 20% by the year 2020 and 26-28% by 2025, with all cuts relative to 2005 emission levels. However, it was president Barrack Obama who agreed this and his last term in office ends January 2017, and his successors may abandon the agreement before it would be fully implemented. This may be especially likely to occur if Obama's successors are Republicans, who have been openly critical of Obama's policies on climate change.

The European Union (EU), together as a set of countries the third largest GHG emitter, agreed a 40% cut in emissions on 1990 levels by the year 2030. But this is only binding on the EU as a whole and there are no targets for any countries individually. And this sets up the situation where the EU countries can blame each other if the target isn't met (Guardian, 2014).

Many people have hope for future climate change agreements, but from past evidence it appears that the biggest GHG emitters, USA, China, and the EU countries, will only agree to GHG emission reductions which they can't be held to. Instead of taking actual action to reduce GHG emissions and improve welfare countries appear to be adopting a cunning strategy, where they claim to work toward this goal while doing very little. In simply terms it looks like they are playing a game with GHG emissions.

The game of cutting greenhouse gas emissions

When one party's actions affect the welfare of others there is said to be strategic interaction, and parties must always adopt a strategy in any interaction to protect their own welfare. This need to adopt a strategy makes all interactions like a game, and game theory is a model specifically designed to represent such scenarios. Game theory simply shows the parties involved in the interaction, known as the 'players' of the game, along with the possible strategies available to each player, and the payoffs each player receives from following each strategy. With players always expected to seek out a higher payoff the game can reveal the likely chosen strategies and the outcome of the interaction, and it can also reveal what would need to change to achieve a different and perhaps more desirable outcome.

It has already been noted above that the problem of global warming requires collective action, and therefore it should be modelled as a collection action game with game theory. In a collective action game the optimum outcome (in this case the reduction of greenhouse gas emissions) is not naturally achieved by self-interested players, but there can be any one of three causes for this:

1) There is agreement over the most desirable outcome, but those involved lack confidence in others and don't believe their behaviour will contribute to that outcome, and this lack of confidence in others results in players following sub-optimal strategies, and gives an unwanted outcome. This is known as an 'assurance' game;

2) There is agreement over the most desirable outcome, but the individual incentives of those involved

sees independent action result in an undesirable outcome. This is known as a 'prisoners' dilemma' game;

3) There is disagreement over the most desirable outcome and those involved have different goals, and the challenge is to avoid a potentially disastrous outcome to the conflict. This is known as a 'chicken' game.

The next three sections look into these three different types of collection action game in turn, to assess how relevant each type of game is to the situation of greenhouse gas emissions cuts, and the prospects each game holds for a likely resolution of the global warming problem.

4.2 Emissions Cuts as an Assurance Game

There is some evidence that the greenhouse gas emitting countries are behaving like they are playing an assurance game. There appears to now be a general agreement on the need to reduce GHG emissions at the highest levels of governments worldwide, as evidenced by global talks on the topic. Yet countries seem to lack confidence that others will cut their own emissions, and this is often the reason given as to why a country wants to delay cutting its own emissions levels until they've seen others contribute to the goal. Representing GHG cuts as an assurance collective action game may therefore be an accurate representation of the real-life situation with global warming, and therefore this type of game may shed some insights on how to motivate countries to proceed and actually cut GHG emissions in the real world.

The following diagram shows the USA and China as the two major players in the game of GHG emission cuts, as they emit more greenhouse gases than any other countries. In the game each of the two players USA and China has a choice of two strategies, to cut emissions or to not cut emissions. When combined with the strategy followed by the other player each of these two choices results in a specific payoff. The four boxes in the diagram show the numerical payoffs associated with the strategy combinations given in the corresponding row and column, with the USA's payoff always the first of the two numbers and China's payoff always the second of the two numbers. For example, if both the USA and China were to cut emissions the applicable payoffs would be those in the top left box, with a payoff of 2 for each country. And if the USA didn't cut emissions but China did the relevant payoffs are those in the bottom left box, with a payoff of 0 for the USA and a negative payoff of -3 for China. But as will soon be explained, the actual numerical values of payoffs don't matter as much as which strategy offers the higher payoff for a country.

An assurance game

		CHINA	
		Cut emissions	Don't cut emissions
USA	Cut emissions	2, 2	-3, 0
	Don't cut emissions	0, -3	-2, -2

In this assurance game if China was to cut emissions (left column in the diagram) then the USA would get a payoff of 0 from not cutting emissions (bottom row first number), but a higher payoff of 2 if they followed suit and also cut emissions (top row first number). The logic behind this is that if only China cuts emissions then the global warming and climate change effect is only reduced not fully resolved (payoff of 0 for USA), while if the USA also cuts emissions then the two largest polluters will have made a statement to reduce GHG emissions. Other GG emitting countries would feel pressure to copy them, to fully resolve the global warming problem for a higher payoff for the USA (payoff of 2). In this assurance game the USA would therefore be expected to cut emissions if China did likewise. And with symmetrical payoffs for the two countries (an assumption made for simplicity) China will cut emissions if the USA can give assurances that it will too.

If China didn't cut GHG emissions (right column in the previous diagram) then the USA would get a payoff of -3 if they cut emissions by themselves (top row third number), and a still negative but higher payoff of -2 if they copied China and also didn't cut emissions (bottom row third number). The logic behind these payoffs is that if neither country cuts emissions then global warming continues unabated (payoff of -2 for the USA). And if only the USA cuts emissions then not only is global warming not fully resolved but the USA also sacrifices economic growth (for a lower payoff of -3), as reducing emissions would naturally require cutting back on productive sectors of its economy. With these payoffs the USA won't cut their GHG emissions if China doesn't, and with symmetrical payoffs China won't cut their emissions if the USA doesn't.

The overall result is that in an assurance game both the USA and China will have the same strategy as the other in their global warming policy. The situation where one country reduces GHG emissions but the other doesn't simply isn't sustainable, as a country will have the incentive to change its strategy to gain a higher payoff (as just explained). Either both cut emissions or neither country cuts them. In this game there are therefore two long-run outcomes, known as Nash equilibriums in game theory, and the first is where both the USA and China cut emissions for positive payoffs of 2 each, while the second Nash equilibrium is where neither the USA nor China cut emissions, for negative payoffs of -2 each. Both of these possible outcomes are underlined in the assurance game diagram.

Dealing with an assurance game

There is both good and bad news if the issue of GHG emission cuts is actually an assurance game in the real world. On the one hand the good news is that the most desired outcome, where the biggest polluters the USA and

China both cut emissions, is a stable long-run equilibrium outcome and it is possible if they could somehow get there. But the bad news is that it is only one of two equilibrium outcomes, and the current real world outcome with neither country taking major steps to reduce emissions is also a stable equilibrium.

The global warming issue has often been treat as an assurance game by GHG emitting countries worldwide, with the focus on just getting states to the position of cutting emissions, confident that they'll stay in that position once they're there. The Kyoto Protocol aimed to do this by getting the most developed countries such as the USA and the EU countries, the earliest industrializers and GHG emitters, to commit to binding emission reductions first, based on the idea that they would incur a lower cost in doing so than less developed countries. With the USA and EU countries committed to low emissions other countries with GHG emissions would, accordingly to the assumptions of an assurance game, soon naturally move toward a strategy to also cut emissions as that would be in their best interests. And the Kyoto Protocol expected wealthier countries such as the USA and EU countries to aid the process by giving billions of dollars in side payments, and supplying technology, to developing countries to facilitate their transition to lower emissions, and cover the significant economic growth losses which GHG cuts may cause.

In practice however treating global warming as an assurance game doesn't seem to work. The second biggest greenhouse gas polluter the USA didn't ratify the Kyoto Protocol, and refused to pay sizable side payments to large GHG emitters such as China, which wasn't given binding targets by the protocol. It appears the USA didn't see binding emission targets as helping it reach a preferred equilibrium outcome, nor did it have faith that other countries would naturally follow any decision to commit to emission cuts, both of which contradict the assumptions of an assurance game. Evidence suggests that another type of game may therefore be required to represent the situation of GHG emission cuts more accurately.

4.3 Emissions Cuts as a Prisoners' Dilemma Game

Empirical evidence may suggest that the second type of collection action game noted in section 4.1, a prisoners' dilemma game, is the most applicable to global warming. Countries may agree that a reduction in greenhouse gas emissions is desirable, but find that their individual incentives ensure that such an outcome remains elusive. The explanations the USA gave for not ratifying the Kyoto treaty support this idea, and the two main reasons given are both related to individual incentives and interests. First, the United States stated that they would not support an international treaty which harmed U.S. economic interests, referring to the fact that the agriculture and industry which caused GHG emissions was also the driver of the United States' economic growth. Second, the USA objected to the lack of emission reduction targets for developing countries, which suggests an awareness that developing countries have (like the USA) an incentive to avoid GHG emission reductions in order to protect their economies, and that external binding targets may be required to overcome this. With individual incentives playing a large role a prisoners' dilemma game may best represent the challenge to cut GHG emissions, and therefore provide the most insight into how to proceed.

The prisoners' dilemma game is named after the theoretical dilemma faced by two prisoners who are being questioned by police. Although the two prisoners would both be better off keeping their mouths shut, to escape with only limited prison time based on what the police can prove and not the full list of crimes they've actually committed, their individual incentives get in the way. Each prisoner has the incentive to throw the other under the bus and play the role of clueless follower to get off scot-free, but with both prisoners doing this the police have all the evidence they need to convict both prisoners on all the crimes they committed. And the prisoners' choice to act as individuals leaves them each worse off than if they had worked together. The prisoners' dilemma game is purely theoretical, but the idea behind it is applicable to a wide range of empirical scenarios.

The following prisoners' dilemma game replicates the assurance game introduced in the last section with the same players, the two biggest sources of GHG emissions China and the USA, and the same strategy options, to cut emissions or to not cut emissions, but with one major difference. All payoffs linked with not cutting emissions are increased by 3 (i.e. a 0 payoff in the assurance game becomes a 3 payoff, and a -2 payoff is now a 1 payoff), due to a greater acknowledgement of the economic benefits a country gains from not having to rework the economy to lower GHG emissions. This counts for both the motivations given by the United States and others for not ratifying the Kyoto treaty, and for the lack of faith in other countries' likelihood of reducing GHG emissions. As in the last game the USA's payoff is always the first of each pair of numbers, and China's payoff is always the second of each pair of numbers.

A prisoners' dilemma game

		CHINA	
		Cut emissions	Don't cut emissions
USA	Cut emissions	2, 2	-3, 3
	Don't cut emissions	3, -3	1, 1

In this example prisoners' dilemma game if China cut their greenhouse gas emissions (left column in the diagram) then the USA would gain a payoff of 2 if they also cut emissions (top row first number). But the USA could get a higher payoff of 3 if they chose the reverse strategy to China and didn't cut emissions (bottom row first number). Therefore if China cut their GHG emissions the USA would be expected to not cut their own, to achieve a higher payoff. And with symmetrical payoffs between the U.S. and China (again assumed for simplicity) the same holds true for China the other way around, and if the USA reduced emissions then China would be expected to do the opposite and not cut their own greenhouse gas emissions.

If China didn't cut their GHG emissions levels (right column in the diagram) then the USA would gain a negative payoff of -3 from doing the opposite and cutting GHG emissions themselves (top row third number). But the U.S. could gain a higher payoff of 1 if they copied China's policy and also didn't cut emissions (bottom row third number). Therefore the USA would be expected to avoid cutting their GHG emissions if that is the path China followed, as such a strategy would earn the United States a higher payoff than doing otherwise. And with symmetrical payoffs China would be expected to not reduce emissions if the USA didn't reduce their own.

No matter the strategy of the other country both China and the USA will not cut their GHG emissions according to this prisoners' dilemma game. Not cutting greenhouse gas emissions is their best reply to any and all behaviour from the other country and offers the highest possible payoff, and it is therefore the dominant strategy of both countries which they would be expected to follow 100% of the time. This gives an expected long-run Nash equilibrium outcome where China and the USA don't cut emissions and receive a payoff of 1 each, and this is underlined in the prisoners' dilemma game diagram. But this result is worse for both countries than if they had each reduced their emissions, where they would have gained a superior payoff of 2 each.

Dealing with a prisoners' dilemma game

The prisoners' dilemma game suggests a bleak picture, where both players suffer a lower payoff than they could have achieved by failing to prioritize cooperation over independently acting on their individual incentives, and where the social optimum with the highest sum of payoffs is not an equilibrium outcome. But there is a solution to a prisoners' dilemma type game, and therefore there may be a solution to the GHG emissions problem if it is as portrayed here in real life with the USA and China. The game above assumes that players only choose their strategy once, and basically assumes a one-off game, but if the game was to be repeated then there is the potential for players to change their behaviour. The basic idea is that each participant in the game would follow a tit-for-tat trigger strategy, and repeat whatever the other player did in the previous round of interaction. Any 'bad' behaviour, i.e. not cutting emissions in this game, would trigger the other player to respond with the same reciprocal bad behaviour of their own at the next available opportunity, and they also wouldn't cut emissions. 'Good' behaviour, i.e. cutting GHG emissions in this game, would also see the other player respond in kind by also cutting emissions. Although not cutting emissions would still be the dominant strategy for each individual round for both players, the players shouldn't look at rounds individually but come to view them as a whole. They should come to realize that under tit-for-tat rules cutting emissions in the current round of interaction guarantees a higher payoff in the next round (2 payoff using payoffs from the example game here), relative to the payoff they would get from not cutting emissions in the current round (1 payoff using payoffs from the example game). And totalling up payoffs from future rounds of interaction should see it in players' interests to cut their GHG emissions, and both the USA and China should act accordingly and do this.

In practice however neither the USA nor China, nor any countries, have adopted a tit-for-tat strategy in the issue of greenhouse gas emissions. The idea that a country would punish others GHG emissions by increasing their own pollution until a lesson is learned seems ridiculous, and is not seen in the global arena. But there is a system of rewards and punishments at the smaller regional level, where the idea of tradable emissions permits has become popular in some areas. The European Union Emission Trading Scheme operates across Europe and uses a cap and trade policy, where a certain level of emissions is given as an allowance for a set period of time. If less

GHGs are emitted than the allowance then the remaining amount can be sold on to others, to financially reward emissions cuts, while emission levels which exceed the allowance are either met with fines or can be bought from others in advance, to financially punish GHG emissions.

The existence of an emissions trading market suggests that the global warming problem is fundamentally different from a prisoners' dilemma game. In such a game the expected Nash equilibrium long-run outcome is where none of the players reduce emissions, and the solution to this problem is to get all participants to cut emissions by other players using tit-for-tat punishment when they don't. However, the result of emissions trading permits is an outcome where some participants cut emissions and others pay to get away with not reducing emissions, completely different from a prisoners' dilemma game. With countries worldwide not treating GHG emissions as a prisoners' dilemma game the next section examines a more accurate alternative model.

4.4 Emissions Cuts as a Chicken Game

Evidence may show the third type of collective action game noted in section 4.1 to be the most relevant to the situation of global warming and greenhouse gas (GHG) emission reduction. This type of game is known as a chicken game where there is disagreement among participants on the most desirable outcome, and the challenge is avoiding a disastrous outcome. There is undoubtedly some disagreement across the globe on the importance of reducing GHG emissions, for a number of reasons. First, there is a minority of sceptics who believe that climate change is a myth, or if it is real that it is not caused by human activity and greenhouse gases but is instead a natural occurrence, and therefore there is no need to cut GHG emissions. Second, even if people believe in man-made global warming the effects of it and climate change will not be distributed equally worldwide, while some areas will also be able to cope better than others. It therefore follows that different people will hold different opinions on the threat posed by global warming, and the importance of addressing it. Third, countries with faster rates of economic growth have more to lose by restructuring their economies to be more environmentally friendly, and are naturally less enthusiastic about the prospect than countries in the world with lower economic growth rates. And the disastrous outcome the chicken game warns of is also clearly present with global warming, and if the mainstream scientific opinion is correct then unchecked GHG emissions at their current level (or higher) will have a terrible effect on the planet and those living on it.

In a chicken game the participant which gets the other side to give in first while holding out themselves receives the highest payoff, while the 'chicken' who gives in first suffers a worse and negative payoff. Even though both players are aware of this fact there is still an individual incentive to give in first in a chicken game, as both players will suffer the worst possible outcome if neither player yields to the other.

The following diagram shows an example chicken game, and as in the previous two game diagrams the players involved are the USA and China, the two biggest greenhouse gas emitters at the current time. As before each player has a choice of two strategies, to reduce their GHG emissions or to not reduce them, but some of the payoffs associated with the strategies have been changed. Most of the payoffs are the same as in the previous prisoners' dilemma game example, with the explanations for the payoffs given earlier, but in order to better represent the calamitous scenario where neither of the two biggest GHG emitters reduce emissions the associated payoffs have been made far worse. A payoff of 1 for each country has been replaced with a payoff of -10, and if neither the USA nor China reduces their enormous GHG emissions then significant climate change is assumed to transpire in the near future, with all of the associated negative effects outlined in section 4.1. It may seem strange to only make this one change to the game's payoffs, and not alter the assumption of symmetric payoffs, when a chicken game appears to revolve around the idea that players hold divergent interests. But this will all be explained in time, and as will be made clear this one change to the payoffs in the event that none of the participants cut emissions completely transforms the game.

A chicken game

		CHINA	
		Cut emissions	Don't cut emissions
USA	Cut emissions	2, 2	-3, 3
	Don't cut emissions	3, -3	-10, -10

If China cut emissions in this example chicken game (left column in the diagram) then the USA would receive a payoff of 2 if they also cut their GHG emissions (top row first number). But the U.S. could achieve a higher payoff of 3 if they did the opposite and didn't cut their emissions (bottom row first number). Therefore if China cuts their greenhouse gas emissions the USA would be expected to do the opposite, and with symmetrical payoffs (again assumed for simplicity) the same holds in the other direction, and if the USA reduces their emissions levels then China won't in this game.

If China didn't cut their GHG emissions (right column in the diagram) then the USA will suffer a negative payoff of -3 if they do the opposite and reduce their own GHGs regardless (top row third number). But the U.S. will receive a far worse negative payoff of -10 if they copy China's strategy and also don't cut their GHG emissions (bottom row third number). Therefore if China doesn't cut emissions in this game then the USA would be expected to do the opposite and reduce their own, and with symmetrical payoffs if the USA doesn't cut GHG emissions then China would cut their own GHG levels in response.

Putting all of these results together reveals that there are two expected Nash equilibrium long-run outcomes in this game, both underlined in the chicken game diagram, where the USA and China follow different strategies and one cuts emissions while the other doesn't. The country which doesn't cut their greenhouse gas levels will gain a positive payoff of 3 as it enjoys the benefits of partially reduced GHG in the atmosphere, for partially reduced climate change effects, without having to make any major sacrifices of its own to lower its own emissions. But the country which does cut its emissions faces a negative payoff of -3, and its economy will suffer from the policies required to cut GHGs and will fall behind on the world stage. And it will have to watch the other major world power's economy benefit and race ahead from doing the opposite, as it carries on polluting the environment.

Dealing with a chicken game

There is some good news if the global warming and climate change issue is actually like a chicken game in the real world. While in the assurance game and prisoners' dilemma game representations of greenhouse gases the worst outcome, where no-one cuts their emissions, is a Nash equilibrium long-run outcome, in the chicken game it is not. In a chicken game between two countries the Nash equilibrium sees one country cut their GHG emissions, and therefore there will be at least some progress on the climate change problem, and effects may be lessened or delayed until further into the future. However, the bad news is that the most desirable outcome where all sides reduce emissions is not a possible long-run outcome in a chicken game, and the game predicts that therefore the climate change problem will never be fully resolved. And unlike the prisoners' dilemma game repeating this game has no prospect of leading to all sides cutting emissions, as here only one side gains a higher payoff from that outcome, and the other side which isn't cutting emissions would actively resist it.

The only way to deal with a chicken game, if that is what the challenge to reduce greenhouse gas emissions essentially represents, is to let it play out, and let the participant who cares the most about the issue be the one to cut their emissions. This is what the European Union Emission Trading Scheme has done by creating a market for GHG emissions. Those who care least about reducing GHGs in Europe, even to the extent that it costs them financially, can simply pay for increased emissions allowances, while those who care most about reducing emissions can do so and sell their allowances to others.

The European Union's decision to start the Emissions Trading Scheme policy could be seen as the result of Europe losing a chicken game with the USA over the Kyoto treaty, as the United States convinced Europe that it wouldn't be following the Kyoto agreement. With the USA apparently committed to not following Kyoto policies to cut emissions, and not coming up with an alternative, the European Union countries were left with a choice. They could either also reject the Kyoto treaty and no-one cuts emissions, which would give Europe a payoff of -10 using the payoffs in the example chicken game, or they could reduce GHG emissions by themselves for a superior payoff of -3 using the example game's payoffs. Europe followed the predictions of a chicken game and did the latter, and the USA won the game as the European Union countries were punished for caring more.

USA vs. China

Returning to the two countries which have been featured in all of the assurance, prisoners' dilemma, and chicken games, the two biggest greenhouse gas emitters in the world the USA and China, their real world behaviour on GHG emissions could also be interpreted as a chicken game. Although the governments of both countries have recently made moves toward a climate change agreement there always appears to be more concern about getting others on board with emissions cuts, instead of setting an example and just doing it themselves. This is perfectly in line with the predictions of the chicken game earlier, where a player seeks to get everyone else to cut emissions while they do the opposite, to get the highest possible payoff. Both the USA and China have also been keen to highlight the obstacles to their country cutting emissions, as if to get across the idea that they can't or won't cut emissions, and it's all down to the other do get it done.

China, like other countries which have seen rapid industrialization over the last few decades, may point to its continuing high growth rates as a reason why it can't cut emissions at the present time, and only in the distant future. The idea is that a focus on reducing greenhouse gases would force sky high economic opportunity costs on the country if implanted now, and that other countries with lower opportunity costs, such as the second highest GHG emitter the USA, should therefore be the ones to cut emissions.

With the Kyoto treaty the USA used a similar argument to the one China now relies upon, and insisted that the United States couldn't implement environmental policies which would harm its economy. But although that reason may have convinced Europe in years past, and saw the USA win a prior chicken game as European Union countries adhered to Kyoto driven GHG emissions cuts while the USA abandoned them, the same strategy may not work with China in what appears to be a new chicken game. Any talk of needing to protect the national economy would imply that the USA could and should cut GHGs before China does, as China has greater economic growth rates and more to lose than the United States in this area. This fact may explain why elected officials in the USA have appeared to move toward the two other strategies mentioned earlier on outcome disagreement, to make a stronger attempt to convince China and the rest of the world that they won't be cutting GHG emissions and others will have to do it instead.

First, there has been evidence of U.S. political officials casting increasing doubt on the scientific evidence of global warming and climate change. One well-publicized example of this was an American Senator using a snowball to try and disprove global warming in the U.S. Senate (TIME, 2015). And second, the U.S. may be trying to get across the idea that they will suffer less from climate change than other countries. An example of this is a Florida Governor banning his employees from using words which would express concern about the issue, and they were forbidden from using words such as 'global warming', 'climate change', and 'sea-level rise' (Guardian, 2015).

Only time will tell whether it will be the USA's or China's strategy which works, and which will convince the rest of the world that they won't be reducing their greenhouse gas emissions and that other countries will have to do it all by themselves. But if the climate change issue is essentially a chicken game then there is sure to be both winners and losers.

5 Cultural Difference

5.1 Communitarianism and Cultural Conflict

Chapter 4 highlighted the problems which may arise when different countries have different outcome preferences, as the superior collective outcome and social optimum is missed, and potential catastrophes such as climate change become possibilities. Communitarians believe that such a scenario is inevitable in the international arena, and like realists communitarians believe that international relations is defined by conflict between nation-states. While realists believe the cause of this conflict is states struggling for relative power gains for its own sake, communitarians go further and see incommensurable cultures as the cause of conflict, and the defining feature of international relations.

Communitarianism defined

Communitarianism believes that people are defined by their cultural identity, and that this will be a national cultural identity. Although a nation-state may contain people following a range of various different cultures they must be brought together in order for a society to function, and communitarianism believes that shared perspectives, values, and customs therefore form in a nation-state to create a national identity and national community. Communitarians argue that once this national identity and set of values is formed it will be vigorously defended in the international arena, as it is the glue which holds the people and the state together. And communitarianism believes a state will naturally seek out power and economic opportunities in the global arena in order to better defend this national identity and values (Brown et al., 2004).

In summary, communitarianism sees culture as having fixed local origins, but yet causing a global impact as it is vociferously defended internationally. This may lead to international competition and conflicts as nation-states attempt to have their own particular values dominate the global system, to ensure that those values can never be threatened and extinguished at the local level of the state. Samuel Huntington's 'Clash of Civilizations' (1996) epitomizes this idea. Referring back to the last chapter and the use of game theory, communitarianism would predict international relations outcomes where one state wins and spreads its culture, and another state loses and its cultural influence is reduced. This result may take the form of a chicken game as explained earlier where one side yields to another, or a simpler 'zero-sum' game where one side's gains are always exactly proportional to another side's losses, and the sum of both sides' payoffs always equals zero.

Empirical evidence supporting communitarianism

There is some evidence supporting the communitarian view that cultural conflict defines international relations, and that states are primarily focused upon defending their own national culture at the expense of others, despite frequent claims to the contrary. For example, the United States has often accused other countries around the world of wrongdoing, and of failing to follow international laws or global norms and instead causing internal or external conflict based on nationalist sentiment. And the USA has often acted as world police in what they have insisted was an attempt to resolve these conflicts. However, the U.S. led wars in Afghanistan and Iraq in 2001 and 2003 respectively went against both international law and international norms (with unprecedented levels of protests) yet the USA proceeded regardless, causing many to see its attitude to international relations as hypocritical. American policy toward Afghanistan and Iraq had also created additional conflict, seemingly in order to acquire oil to fund the consumerist U.S. culture, and to expand U.S. geopolitical influence in the region to increase American power internationally, and better protect against any threats to U.S. global dominance and their national way of life.

Another example supporting communitarian ideas is the clash between the West and the East on issues such as workers' rights. The West has often criticized developing Eastern countries such as India, China and other states in East Asia for their poor working conditions, and the lack of adequate rights for employees. But although Western critics may insist that their motives for speaking out are benevolent and based on the idea of universal human rights, many in the East suspect that less altruistic motives are at play. People in Eastern countries may insist that long work hours without breaks and employees showing self-sacrifice for the greater good are simply examples of Asian values, which are the driving force behind the rapid economic growth their countries have enjoyed in recent decades. And that Western criticism of these habits is simply an attempt to undermine the foundations responsible for Asian success, to weaken the West's competitors on the international stage. If this really is the true motive behind Western concerns then it backs communitarianism and the idea that Western countries are simply seeking to preserve their own cultural values, by weakening rival countries which could threaten them at some point in the future. And seeking to eliminate successful alternative values which could ultimately grow and replace them in their own countries. And even if Western criticism of practices in the East has genuinely good intentions, those who defend the practices with talk of 'Asian values' are also supporting the ideas of communitarians, by wanting to defend and preserve what they see as their local fixed culture, and discourage the spread of Western alternatives.

5.2 Constructivism and Cultural Change

While communitarianism views culture as fundamentally fixed and local the constructivist view of international relations disagrees. Constructivism predicts different prospects for international order and argues that cultural difference between countries need not result in conflict, but can instead lead to mutual cultural change.

Constructivism defined

Constructivists agree with communitarians that culture defines interactions between nation-states in the global system, but the similarities end there. Constructivism doesn't believe culture to be fixed but instead sees it as something which changes over time, as states' interests evolve and their identities and roles are transformed. This is a similar process to that put forward earlier with liberal international theory, but instead of being driven by changes in dominant groups within a country constructivism sees changes in social perceptions as the driving factor. Constructivists such as Wendt sum it up best by describing culture, and the international relations between states which follows from culture, as a social construction. The idea is that interactions between states change both internal and external perceptions of a society, which in turn changes national values and the national identity, to construct a new set of values.

According to constructivism the interactions between states lead to a process of cultural change in one of two ways. First, nation-states may adopt and then convey selected values found within their borders, to demonstrate common values with another state to form a more rewarding association with each other. Second, nation-states may simply fabricate values which they don't possess to create a more favourable public image and identity, which can support the goal of achieving more beneficial relationships with other states. Either way, constructivists believe that the construction of these historical and social common values strengthens a nation-state's position on the international stage, which in turn supports recognition and reinforcement of a state's sovereignty, and protects a nation-state's national culture. And these benefits associated with adopting common international values ensures that a state will continue with the process, to enshrine cultural change into the culture of the nation-state (Brown et al., 2004).

In summary, constructivism sees culture as fluid and not fixed, as states modify and change their culture to better manage interactions with other states on the global stage. As foreign influences are thought to have the potential to change a country's culture constructivists naturally believe that culture has both local and global origins. The changes constructivists predict can be either positive or negative, and constructivists believe that cultural difference does have the potential to offer mutual benefits for nation-states, instead of merely conflict where one side wins at the other's expense as communitarianism predicts. Referring back to the last chapter and the use of game theory, constructivism may predict the international relations outcomes associated with an assurance game. More than one long-run outcome is possible, but nation-states can gain a better outcome by forging greater trust and alliances with other states.

Empirical evidence supporting constructivism

There are various examples supporting constructivist theory, and the idea that interactions between nation-states are not a fight for cultural and national supremacy but see the construction of values and cultural change on both sides. One example is the increased international trade, tourism, and communication interaction between nation-states in recent decades, as states have emphasized their best qualities to other nations and forged lucrative associations as a result. Increased international trade allows citizens in many countries to eat various foods out of season, and have access to a wide range of goods from across the globe; tourism allows travel across the world to almost any country a citizen may choose; and international communication gives access to foreign citizens and media for new information, perspectives or entertainment. This trade, tourism, and communication hasn't necessarily resulted in one nation-state trying to conquer another, and it simply opens up greater cultural choices to one nation-state's consumers, and greater profits to another nation-state's producers/sellers, offering mutual benefits to both sides in the interaction.

More evidence supporting constructivism, albeit a more negative example to show that socially constructed outcomes will not always be beneficial, is based on the results of USA led military efforts in the Middle East. These wars have not resulted in one country (e.g. the United States) imposing its culture on another, but have instead seen cultural change on both sides. Countries such as Iraq are certainly not following the culture of the United States, but they have seen cultural change as the rulers and policies of their states have been reconstructed. And the USA has also changed following the 21st century war in Iraq, as an unintended consequence of the war has been the rise of Islamic extremist group ISIS (Islamic State of Iraq and Syria), also known as ISIL (Islamic State of Iraq and the Levant). The Iraq war and removal of Saddam Hussein left a power vacuum in the country which ISIS filled, and the radical group has expanded outwards since then and constructed a powerful and ruthless image of terror, with its crimes including the beheadings of American (and other nationalities') journalists and aid workers. This has forced U.S. culture to change to manage the new threat and the associated propaganda, and the changes have seen some Americans eliminate various Muslim countries from their vacation destinations, while others have simply adopted a stronger pro-war or pro-free speech attitude to try and defy ISIS's goals. In this example greater interactions between states hasn't brought a beneficial cultural change, but instead has increased animosity for the other side and changed cultures for the worse.

5.3 Cosmopolitanism and Cultural Unity

The final theory on the role of cultural difference in international relations is given by cosmopolitanism, which goes further than constructivism and essentially represents the opposite of communitarianism.

Cosmopolitanism defined

While communitarians believe that cultural difference between nation-states will inevitably result in cultural conflict as states fight it out for cultural dominance, and constructivists see cultural difference as forcing cultural change via state interaction, cosmopolitanism is more optimistic. Cosmopolitanism believes that cultural difference doesn't have to result in one nation-state's culture being dominated and eliminated, or even just changed, but sees a world where different cultures can coexist exactly as they are. This is made possible due to the cosmopolitan belief than all people across all cultures worldwide share some important common values. With cosmopolitanism the idea is that states won't need to fight among themselves, or try to construct a certain image to other states, and they can instead rely on supranational organizations or ideas which will serve a universally shared ideal (Brown et al., 2004).

In the cosmopolitan understanding of international relations nation-states are not necessarily the foremost unit of international order, and global governance can become more than just a sphere for states to interact with each other and be a leading sphere in its own right. With cosmopolitanism theory states are not attempting to defend their national culture and community by forcing it on other states (as in communitarianism), nor attempting to forge lucrative associations with other states by constructing an appealing narrative of their own values (as with constructivism), but they instead watch out for deviations from global norms. If a state is thought to deviate from widely accepted global norms then other nation-states – irrespective of their national culture and the cultural difference between them – are thought to get together in an attempt to bring the problem state into line.

In summary, cosmopolitanism sees a world where cosmopolitan cultural difference at the local national level is protected by a shared belief in fixed global norms. States don't interact with each other so much as they evaluate different nation-states on the extent to which they follow those global norms and universal values. Referring back to the last chapter and game theory, cosmopolitanism would predict international relations outcomes related to a prisoners' dilemma type game. And while states may have an individual incentive to abandon global values and instead screw rival states over in some way to gain a superior national payoff, cosmopolitanism believes that mechanisms are in place to prevent this coming to pass in the long-run. Either supranational global organizations are thought to take away state power to act on these incentives, or other nation-states are thought to discourage acting on them by threatening tit-for-tat reciprocal behaviour of their own if global ideals and norms are violated.

Empirical evidence supporting cosmopolitanism

Just like the other two theories examined earlier there is also some evidence supporting the cosmopolitan view of international relations, that global institutions or ideals can take priority over nation-states' different cultures on the global stage. The United Nations (UN) and the International Criminal Court (ICC) are examples of supranational organizations which have taken on a leading role in international relations, and in doing so partly reduced some of the problems and issues associated with states dealing with each other directly. The ICC targets serious international criminals across the globe, to reduce states' need to dominate rival states to protect against this (as in communitarianism). And the UN works to forge better relationships between countries on important issues, to reduce the need for nation-states to misrepresent themselves to others for this end (as in constructivism).

However, many critics of the United Nations and International Criminal Court, and supranational organizations in general, argue that they don't really represent a cosmopolitan world where global governance supersedes nation-states, but are instead representations of Western and especially American interests. The argument being that the UN and ICC tends to only focus on issues and go after criminals in less powerful poorer countries, but have looked the other way and done nothing when similar issues and serious criminals occur in the more powerful West, and especially the United States. But it can also be said that in the West serious issues or international criminals are often dealt with internally by states, while outside the West in countries with a weaker infrastructure this may not be the case, and this is why the UN or ICC need to step in. Using this understanding supranational organizations such as the United Nations and International Criminal Court play a vital role, and they will only focus upon the states which don't address important issues or tackle international criminals themselves, which gives an incentive for states to keep their house in order. This supports the ideas of cosmopolitanism and cultural difference at the level of the nation-state coexisting with a set of global values.

Perhaps the strongest supporter of cosmopolitanism is the increasing focus on the idea of universal human rights over recent decades, and criticism of other countries' policies is increasingly undertaken using the language of human rights values. There is a focus on how a change in another state's policies would protect a persecuted group and support the goal of advancing human rights, while open nationalist language about what a nation-state gains by changing a rival state's policies is less common than it used to be. This may represent more of a move toward cosmopolitism in international relations.

Those who are sceptical of cosmopolitan theory may say that talk of human rights abuses in foreign countries is simply a politically correct cover for Western states, which may be accused of following a nationalist communitarian policy despite claiming otherwise. However, even if this is true it does not necessarily disprove cosmopolitanism, as all states (and aspiring states) are increasingly using the language of human rights and claiming to believe in the global value of universal human rights. Countries such as Russia and China have been criticized for their human rights violations by the USA, as have extremist Muslim terror groups which aspire to statehood, but the response has increasingly been to simply reverse the allegations. Russian and Chinese media have pointed out that the United States has a highly flawed human rights record when dealing with its own citizens, especially those of ethnic minority backgrounds. And individuals found guilty of belonging to radical Muslim terror groups and performing terrorist acts have also played the global human rights card, and insisted that their acts were simply a reprisal against American and Western human rights abuses in their homelands during foreign wars. This last example suggests that shared global values are not necessarily always a good thing which should be sought after, as they have the potential to be used as a ready-made excuse and justification for some of the most terrible atrocities seen across the world.

Bibliography

Bromley, S., Mackintosh, M., Brown, W. and Wuyts, M. (eds) (2004) *Making the International: Economic Interdependence and Political Order*, London, Pluto Press.

Brown, W., Bromley, S., and Athreye, S. (eds) (2004) *Ordering the International: History, Change and Transformation*, London, Pluto Press.

Foreign Affairs (2014) *NAFTA's Mixed Record: The View from Mexico*
www.foreignaffairs.com/articles/140351/jorge-g-castaneda/naftas-mixed-record

Guardian (2015) *Republicans' New Climate Strategy: Just Ban the Words 'Climate Change'*
www.theguardian.com/commentisfree/2015/mar/11/republican-new-climate-change-strategy-ban-words-climate-change

Guardian (2014) *US and China Strike Deal On Carbon Cuts in Push for Global Climate Change Pact*
www.theguardian.com/environment/2014/nov/12/china-and-us-make-carbon-pledge

Observatory of Economic Complexity (2014) *Mexico Profile*
http://atlas.media.mit.edu/profile/country/mex/

TIME (2015) *Senator Throws Snowball! Climate Change Disproven!*
http://time.com/3725994/inhofe-snowball-climate/